DEDICATION

To the men and women who have fought for our freedom

ACKNOWLEDGMENTS

I thank Nature's God our Creator for inspiring these men to write these books, and the men for writing the books as well as others who are fighting for our freedom.

Neil Mammen

Jesus Is Involved In Politics! Why Aren't You? Why Isn't Your Church?

Tim LaHaye and David Noebel

Mind Siege: The Battle for Truth in the New Millennium

George Grant

The Family Under Siege: What the New Social Engineers Have in Mind for You and Your Children

Lee Strobel

The Case for Christ: A Journalist's Personal Investigation of the Evidence for Jesus

Samuel Blumenfeld

NEA: Trojan Horse in American Education

Paul Craig Roberts and Lawrence M. Stratton

The Tyranny of Good Intentions: How Prosecutors and Law Enforcement Are Trampling the Constitution in the Name of Justice

Jonathan West

Good-bye America?

Pastor Matthew J. Trewhella

The Doctrine of the Lesser Magistrates: A Proper Resistance to Tyranny and a Repudiation of Unlimited Obedience to Civil Government

Dr. Karl I. Payne
Spiritual Warfare

Christians, Demonization, and Deliverance

Table of Contents

1

USSR of America

> Happy is the man that findeth wisdom, and the man that getteth understanding. For the merchandise of it is better than the merchandise of silver, and the gain thereof than fine gold. She is more precious than rubies: and all the things thou canst desire are not to be compared unto her. Proverbs 3:13–1

Let's look at some wisdom from Scripture and hope we can get some understanding.

> Take away the dross from silver, and there shall come forth a vessel for the finer. Take away the wicked from before the king, and his throne shall be established in righteousness. Proverbs 25:4–5

"Dross" represents impurities, the undesirable stuff that is in the silver. So you need to condition the silver before it goes to the silversmith for jewelry. Therefore, our legislators should be conditioned before we vote them in office.

> The fear of the Lord is the beginning of wisdom: and the knowledge of the holy is understanding. Proverbs 9:10

This is why we should only elect men who fear God and have the knowledge of the holy. **When the righteous are in authority, the people rejoice: but when the wicked beareth rule, the people groan. Proverbs 29:2**

USSR of America

Ask the bakers, florists, photographers, and preachers who are being persecuted for their religious beliefs, "Are you groaning?"

What you should know about the Devil.

Satan can blind people's mind.

He is the god of this world.

> But if our gospel be hid, it is hid to them that are lost: in whom the god of this world hath blinded the minds of them which believe not, lest the light of the glorious gospel of Christ, who is the image of God, should shine unto them. 2 Corinthians 4:3

Satan can corrupt people's mind.

> But I fear, lest somehow, as the serpent deceived Eve by his craftiness, so your minds may be corrupted from the simplicity that is in Christ. 2 Corinthians 11:3

Satan can enter into people

> Then Satan entered Judas, surnamed Iscariot, who was numbered among the twelve. Luke:22:3

Satan's demons can enter into people.

> Jesus asked him, saying, "What is your name?" And he said, "Legion," because many demons had entered him.Luke 8:301

> Be sober , be vigilant ; because your adversary the devil, as a roaring lion, walketh about , seeking whom he may devour:1 Peter 5:8

USSR of America

Put on the whole armor of God, that you may be able to stand against the wiles of the devil.Ephesians 6:11

So the great dragon was cast out, that serpent of old, called the Devil and Satan, who deceives the whole world; he was cast to the earth, and his angels were cast out with him. Rev.12:9

Is there any evidence that Satan has corrupted people's minds from the simplicity that is in Christ?

Is there any evidence that Satan has deceived people?

Let's look an example.

Government: over 18 trillion dollars in debt.

We are robbing the present and future generations.

Inalienable Rights: We have a right to learn and acquire an education, but we don't have a right to be provided an education. We have a right to provide for our families, but we don't have a right to be provided for.

How can God bless our public schools when they are payed for with stolen money?

How can God bless the welfare recipients for using stolen money?

USSR of America

How can God bless our nation when we let our legislators legislate goods, which is stealing.

> If you love me, keep My commandments.
> John 14:15

> "You shall not steal"
> "You shall not murder"
> "You shall not commit adultery"

Why is stealing and murdering allowed by the people?

Kevin Hogan in his book *The Psychology of Persuasion* says that 85% of the people are conformists. I believe that it's just easer for the conformists to believe and justify they are to obey governments and not God.

> 3 For rulers are not a terror to good works, but to the evil. Wilt thou then not be afraid of the power? Do that which is good, and thou shalt have praise of the same: 4 For he is the minister of God to thee for good. Romans 13:

Rulers are to do good, but when rulers become bad and demand what God forbids and forbids what God demands they are not to be obeyed.
https://lessermagistrate.com/

Why did Daniel get thrown into the lion's den?

Why did Shadrach, Meshach, and Abednego get thrown into the fiery furnace?

Why was Apostle Paul let down in the basket over the wall?

USSR of America

Paul was resisting arrest from the authorities.
If we are to obey bad rulers then America should revert back to England and we should be under English law, because our forefathers had no right to revolt.

This next scripture is very serious and I believe it's why America is under God's wrath today.

> 13 For such are false apostles, deceitful workers, transforming themselves into the apostles of Christ. 14 And no marvel; for Satan himself is transformed into an angel of light. 15 Therefore it is no great thing if his ministers also be transformed as the ministers of righteousness; whose end shall be according to their works. 2 Corinthians 11:13

I believe most pastors are conformist and if they preach the true purpose of God they would look bad. How could anyone not want to lobby to take care of the hungry children?

I believe some pastors are false apostles and deceitful workers.

We see people who confess Jesus with their mouth and lobby for socialism. A christian that supports socialism and Planned Parenthood should study 2 Corinthians 13:5 very carefully.

> Examine yourselves as to whether you are in the faith. Test yourselves. Do you not know ourselves, that Jesus Christ is in you?--unless indeed you are disqualified.

9 Know ye not that the unrighteous shall not inherit the kingdom of God? Be not deceived : neither fornicators, nor idolaters, nor adulterers, nor effeminate, nor abusers of themselves with mankind, 10 **Nor thieves**, nor covetous, nor drunkards, nor revilers, nor extortioners, shall inherit the kingdom of God.1 Corinthians 6:9

For whom the Lord loveth he chasteneth , and scourgeth every son whom he receiveth . 7 If ye endure chastening, God dealeth with you as with sons; for what son is he whom the father chasteneth not? 8 But if ye be without chastisement, whereof all are partakers, then are ye bastards, and not sons. 9 Furthermore we have had fathers of our flesh which corrected us, and we gave them reverence : shall we not much rather be in subjection unto the Father of spirits, and live? Hebrews: 12:6-9

Do you believe the Devil is alive and working today?

Why are the unrighteous in authority?

For we wrestle not against flesh and blood, but against principalities, against powers, against the rulers of the darkness of this world, against spiritual wickedness in high places. Ephesians 6:12

Satan is attempting to use high places, such as government, education, organizations, and the media to remove God from the world. Anywhere there is control or influence, Satan's spiritual wickedness is there.

USSR of America

Let's look at the US debt—over $18 trillion. That is more than $57,000 per citizen and $154,000 per taxpayer. http://www.usdebtclock.org

Why would normal people do this?

Why are we in debt?

Satan knows that in order to get the people to consent to change, he needs to create a crisis. So he creates a financial crisis to get people to consent to more government control. The more crises Satan creates, the more consent of the people for government control.

How is Satan doing this?

> And no marvel; for Satan is transformed into an angel of light. Therefore it is no great thing if his ministers also be transformed as the ministers of righteousness; whose end shall be according to their works. 2 Corinthians 11:14–15

We think of "angel" as righteousness without wrong. And "light" brings to mind the notion that without light there is no vision. We might be tempted to see this "righteousness" like the fruit Eve saw in the garden. It might seem desirable but lead to destruction.

Without the wisdom and knowledge of the holy, we will be deceived by the old Serpent called the Devil. Satan's ministers of "righteousness" are striving to control the government, education, media, TV, radio, and publishing.

Why are they doing this?

Satan's ministers of "righteousness" are a deceived people, Satan is trying to use deceived people to remove

USSR of America

God from our society.They cannot believe the Gospel because they are under the power of Satan with demonic blinders. It's not their fault—they have no control over it. Please read ***Praying Effectively for the Lost*** By Lee E. Thomas pelministries.org and you will see why we need to pray for the lost to remove the demonic blinders.

Organizations: Spiritual Wickedness in High Places

AMERICAN HUMANIST ASSOCIATION (AHA)

The American Humanist Association was founded in 1941 and currently provides legal assistance to defend the constitutional rights of secular and religious minorities,[2] actively lobbies Congress on church-state separation and other issues,[3] and maintains a grassroots network of 150 local affiliates and chapters that engage in social activism, philosophical discussion and community-building events.[4] The AHA has several publications, including the bi-monthly magazine The Humanist, a quarterly newsletter Free Mind, a peer-reviewed semi-annual scholastic journal Essays in the Philosophy of Humanism, and a weekly Internet magazine Humanist Network News.[5]
https://en.wikipedia.org/wiki/ikipedia:
Text_of_Creative_Commons_Attribution-
hareAlike_3.0_Unported_License

The Humanist is striving to bring about a progressive society without God. To bring about a progressive society," the humanist seems to believe he must remove God from our society. I believe progressive society is just another term for communist society.

USSR of America

We hold these truths to be self-evident, that all men are created equal, that they are endowed by their Creator with certain unalienable Rights, that among these are Life, Liberty and the pursuit of Happiness." —The Declaration of Independence

In a progressive society, man is not created equal and the ruling authority determines your rights, and we have seen from history that some people have the right to life, liberty, and the pursuit of happiness, and some don't.

Please read *Mind Siege: The Battle for Truth in the New Millennium* By Tim LaHaye and David Noebel

AMERICAN CIVIL LIBERTIES UNION   (ACLU)

They are against the teaching of creationism in public schools and for separation of church and state. Support same-sex marriage and the right of gays to adopt; supporting birth control and abortion rights. Like most of Satan's deception there will be some good to cover the evil. I believe the ACLU is Satan's legal arm to force a God-less, immoral and conscious-less society.
Read *Family under Siege*: by George E. Grant

Satan uses television, publishing, movies, music, and video games to cultivate the minds of the people, and we *can* do something about it.

> Be not deceived: evil communications corrupt good manner. Awake to righteousness, and sin not; for some have not the knowledge of God: I speak this to your shame.1 Corinthians 15:33

It is a shame, and a shame that we don't have the knowledge of God in our churches.

USSR of America

"We the People of the United States, in Order to form a more perfect Union, establish Justice, insure domestic Tranquility, provide for the common defense, promote the general Welfare, and secure the Blessings of Liberty to ourselves and our Posterity, do ordain and establish this Constitution for the United States of America." — Preamble of the Constitution

How can the evil on television, movies, and magazines ensure domestic tranquility, promote the general welfare, and secure the blessing of liberty to ourselves? Remember, "evil communications corrupt good manner.

> For Jerusalem is ruined, and Judah is fallen: because their tongue and their doings are against the Lord, to provoke the eyes of His glory. The shew of their countenance doth witness against them; and they declare their sin as Sodom, they hide it not. Woe unto their soul! for they have rewarded evil unto themselves. Say ye to the righteous, that it shall be well with him: for they shall eat the fruit of their doings. Woe unto the wicked! it shall be ill with him: for the reward of his hands shall be given him. As for my people, children are their oppressors, and women rule over them. O my people, they which lead thee cause thee to err, and destroy the way of thy paths. Isaiah 3:8–12

PLANNED PARENTHOOD FEDERATION OF AMERICA (PPFA)

Planned Parenthood Federation of America (PPFA), commonly shortened to simply Planned Parenthood, is the US affiliate of the International Planned Parenthood Federation (IPPF) and one of its larger members. PPFA provides reproductive health, maternal, and child health services. Planned Parenthood Action Fund (PPAF) is a related organization that lobbies the US political system for prochoice legislation, comprehensive sex education, and access to affordable health care. *https://en.wikipedia.org/wiki/ Wikipedia:Text_of_Creative_Commons_Attribution-ShareAlike_3.0_Unported_License*

I believe Planned Parenthood is Satan's tool for destroying the United States with sexual immorality, and we are letting the organization cultivate the minds of our children in school. The organization's status is as the country's leading provider of surgical abortions.

Where no law is, there is no transgression. Romans 4:15

So in a lawless society, it's OK to kill the unwanted.

SEXUALITY INFORMATION AND EDUCATION COUNCIL OF THE UNITED STATES (SIECUS)

"The Sexuality Information and Education Council of the United States was founded in 1964 by Dr. Mary S. Calderone and a number of other brave pioneers. During her tenure as the Medical Director for the Planned Parenthood Federation, Dr. Calderone became concerned about the lack of accurate information about sexuality for both young people and adults." (Source: siecus.org)

Dr. Calderone was declared "humanist of the year" in 1974 by the American Humanist Association.

NATIONAL EDUCATION ASSOCIATION (NEA)

"The National Education Association (NEA) is the largest labor union in the United States. It represents public school teachers and other support personnel, faculty and staffers at colleges and universities, retired educators, and college students preparing to become teachers. The NEA has just under 3 million members and is headquartered in Washington. The NEA had a budget of more than $341 million for the 2012–2013 fiscal year." *https://en.wikipedia.org/wiki/ Wikipedia:Text_of_Creative_Commons_Attribution- ShareAlike_3.0_Unported_License*

According to author Samuel Blumenfeld, "The NEA's stand on most issues is virtually identical with the radical left. In fact, the NEA seems to have become the main channel through which the radical left is exercising its influence. Those of us who still believe in freedom ought to be very worried, for the NEA controls virtually every school in America through its member-teachers, and those who control the schools control the future." Please read *NEA: Trojan Horse in American Education* By Samuel Blumenfeld

 Satan's ministers has gained control of another organization. When the NEA get a national curriculum to be imposed on all schools, including private, they will have total control of cultivating the minds of the people.

"The hand that rocks the cradle is the hand that rules the world." —poet William Ross Wallace

USSR of America

"Man's mind may be likened to a garden, which may be intelligently cultivated or allowed to run wild; but whether cultivated or neglected, it must, and will, bring forth. If no useful seeds are put into it, then an abundance of useless weed-seeds will fall therein, and will continue to produce their kind." —from *As a Man Thinketh*, by James Allen

The question is, who is going to cultivate our minds?

OTHER ORGANIZATIONS

- United Nations (UN)United Nations Educational,

- Scientific and Cultural Organization (UNESCO)

- World Health Organization (WHO)

- United Nations Children's Fund (UNICEF)

The humanists' main objective is a socialist one-world government without God.

What should we do?

First, preachers must be able to testify as Paul does. Wherefore, I take you to record this day, that I am pure from the blood of all men. For I have not shunned to declare unto you all the counsel of God. Take heed therefore unto yourselves, and to all the flock, over the which the Holy Ghost hath made you overseers, to feed the church of God, which He hath purchased with His own blood. Acts 20:26–28

USSR of America

What is the whole purpose of God?

> For this purpose the Son of God was manifested, that he might destroy the works of the devil. 1 John 3:8

How are we going to share the Gospel to these organizations?

If the preacher could testify as Paul, then there would be no need for this message, for the churches would be declaring the whole purpose of God.

Should the church have the same purpose as the Son of God, to destroy the works of the Devil?

> Jesus warned, He that is not with me is against me; and he that gathereth not with me scattereth abroad. Matthew 12:30
> Jesus sent Paul, To open their eyes, and to turn them from darkness to light, and from the power of Satan unto God, that they may receive forgiveness of sins, and inheritance among them which are sanctified by faith that is in me. Acts 26:18

> But I fear, lest by any means, as the serpent beguiled Eve through his subtlety, so your minds should be corrupted from the simplicity that is in Christ. 2 Corinthians 11:3

When we uncorrupt our minds and understand the simplicity that is in Christ, we will know how to destroy the works of Satan. *Whom we preach, warning every man, and teaching every man in all wisdom; that we may present every man perfect in Christ Jesus.* Colossians 1:28

USSR of America

What part of teaching every man in all wisdom don't we understand?

> Take away the dross from silver, and there shall come forth a vessel for the finer. Take away the wicked from before the king, and his throne shall be established in righteousness. Proverbs 25:4

We should only elect a conditioned person, who has wisdom and understanding, to any government office.

> The fear of the Lord is the beginning of wisdom: and the knowledge of the holy is understanding. Proverbs 9:10

What happens when we remove the wicked from Congress?

> When the righteous are in authority, the people rejoice: but when the wicked beareth rule, the people mourn. Proverbs 29:2

What happens when we do nothing?

> His lord answered and said unto him, Thou wicked and slothful servant, thou knewest that I reap where I sowed not, and gather where I have not strawed:Thou oughtest therefore to have put my money to the exchangers, and then at my coming I should have received mine own with usury. Take therefore the talent from him, and give it unto him which hath ten talents. For unto every one that hath shall be given, and he shall have abundance: but from him that hath not shall be taken away even that which he hath. And cast ye the unprofitable

servant into outer darkness: there shall be weeping and gnashing of teeth. Matthew 25:26–30

Ask the bakers, florists, photographers, preachers, and others who have been persecuted for their religious beliefs, "Are you groaning ?"

Why do the humanists and atheists want to remove God from our society?

Let's look at our Declaration of Independence, transcribed here: "In Congress, July 4, 1776. The unanimous Declaration of the thirteen United States of America: When in the Course of human events, it becomes necessary for one people to dissolve the political bands which have connected them with another, and to assume among the powers of the earth, the separate and equal station to which the Laws of Nature and of Nature's God entitle them, a decent respect to the opinions of mankind requires that they should declare the causes which impel them to the separation. We hold these truths to be self-evident, that all men are created equal, that they are endowed by their Creator with certain unalienable Rights, that among these are Life, Liberty and the pursuit of Happiness.—That to secure these rights, Governments are instituted among Men, deriving their just powers from the consent of the governed,

Without God, would the people have a right to separate from the ruling authority? We see that our governments are instituted to protect our unalienable rights, and we get these rights from the "Laws of Nature and of Nature's God," our Creator.

USSR of America

That whenever any Form of Government becomes destructive of these ends, it is the Right of the People to alter or to abolish it, and to institute new Government, laying its foundation on such principles and organizing its powers in such form, as to them shall seem most likely to effect their Safety and Happiness.

If we remove the laws of nature and of nature's God, our Creator, we will not have any unalienable rights to life, liberty, and the pursuit of happiness. We get our rights from God, not man. Satan is using the humanists as his ministers of righteousness to remove God from our society, to remove our unalienable rights.

We read, "Whenever any Form of Government becomes destructive of these ends, it is the Right of the People to alter or to abolish it, and to institute new Government."

The question then is, do we "The People" have just cause to alter or abolish our government and institute new government?

Is an unborn baby a human being?

If it's a human being, then we "The People" have the right to alter or abolish our government because our government is denying the right to life.

Is stealing against the Laws of Nature and of Nature's God?

If stealing is against the laws of nature and of nature's God, then we "The People" have the right to alter or abolish our government because there is a difference between rights and goods. Our governments are instituted to protect our rights, not legislate goods and give to others.

Socialism and communism are stealing and are against the laws of nature and of nature's God. Only governments that have no laws of nature and of nature's God, our Creator, can deny life and legislate goods.

Where there is no law, there is no transgression.

I believe this is the reason the American Humanist Association, American Civil Liberties Union, and other progressive organizations are trying to remove God from society. I believe, "Progressive" is just another name for "socialist" or "communist."

What happens when a society turns from God and follows Satan's ministers of righteousness?

I'm glad you asked. Well, maybe you didn't ask—but I would like for you to know.

> For the wrath of God is revealed from heaven against all ungodliness and unrighteousness of men, who hold the truth in unrighteousness. Romans 1:18

What is the wrath of God?

> For this cause God gave them up unto vile affections: for even their women did change the natural use into that which is against nature: And likewise also the men, leaving the natural use of the woman, burned in their lust one toward another; men with men working that which is unseemly, and receiving in themselves that

recompence of their error which was meet. And even as they did not like to retain God in their knowledge, God gave them over to a reprobate mind, to do those things which are not convenient; Being filled with all unrighteousness, fornication, wickedness, covetousness, maliciousness; full of envy, murder, debate, deceit, malignity; whisperers, Backbiters, haters of God, despiteful, proud, boasters, inventors of evil things, disobedient to parents, Without understanding, covenant breakers, without natural affection, implacable, unmerciful: Who knowing the judgment of God, that they which commit such things are worthy of death, not only do the same, but have pleasure in them that do them.
Romans 1:26–32

Now you know what the wrath of God is, so when you hear of mass murders, inventors of evil things like pipe bombs and pressure-cooker bombs, and same-sex marriage, you know God's wrath is on America.

How should we deter all ungodliness and unrighteousness of men?

We need to get the humanist, atheist, ACLU, and Planned Parenthood to stop cultivating the minds of the people with all ungodliness and unrighteousness.

How should we do it?

We should get the preachers to testify as Paul to deter the works of the Devil.

Wherefore, I take you to record this day, that I am pure from the blood of all men. For I have not shunned to declare unto you all the counsel of God. Take heed therefore unto yourselves, and to all the flock, over the which the Holy Ghost hath made you overseers, to feed the church of God, which He hath purchased with His own blood. Acts 20:26–28

For this purpose the Son of God was manifested, that he might destroy the works of the devil. 1 John 3:8

The preachers and churches are not doing what they are supposed to, and therefore our rights and freedom are taken away as we experience the wrath of God. Remember "thou wicked and slothful servant"

For unto every one that hath shall be given and he shall have abundance: but from him that hath not shall be taken away even that which he hath. Matthew 25:29

Let's look again at the preamble of our Constitution: "We the People of the United States, in Order to form a more perfect Union, establish Justice, insure domestic Tranquility, provide for the common defence, promote the general Welfare, and secure the Blessings of Liberty to ourselves and our Posterity, do ordain and establish this Constitution for the United States of America."

The preamble states what the Constitution is for.

What is just about all ungodliness and unrighteousness of men?

USSR of America

What is just about stealing?

What is just about $18 trillion in debt?

How can $18 trillion in debt be a liberty to us and future generations, when a borrower is a slave to the lender?

How can the evil on television, in movies, and in magazines, along with the teaching of ungodliness and unrighteousness in our schools, ensure domestic tranquility, promote the general welfare, and secure the blessing of liberty to ourselves?

Remember, "evil communications corrupt good manners."

"Man's mind may be likened to a garden, which may be intelligently cultivated or allowed to run wild; but whether cultivated or neglected, it must, and will, bring forth. If no useful seeds are put into it, then an abundance of useless weed-seeds will fall therein, and will continue to produce their kind. Just as a gardener cultivates his plot, keeping it free from weeds, and growing the flowers and fruits which he requires, so may a man tend the garden of his mind, weeding out all the wrong, useless, and impure thoughts, and cultivating toward perfection the flowers and fruits of right, useful, and pure thoughts. By pursuing this process, a man sooner or later discovers that he is the master-gardener of his soul, the director of his life. He also reveals, within himself, the laws of thought, and understands, with ever-increasing accuracy, how the thought-forces and mind elements operate in the shaping of his character, circumstances, and destiny." — from *As a Man Thinketh*, by James Allen

USSR of America

Who is doing the cultivating, and what types of seeds are being planted into the gardens of our minds?

We see how the thought forces and mind elements operate in the shaping of man's character, circumstances, and destiny. We let our enemies market evil and do nothing about it.

Now we are the USSR of America.

United States Socialist Republic of America.

> If my people, which are called by my name, shall humble themselves, and pray, and seek my face, and turn from their wicked ways; then will I hear from heaven, and will forgive their sin, and will heal their land. 2 Chronicles 7:14
>
> Do you see the part "turn from their wicked ways"?
>
> " When good men do nothing, they are no longer good. Many have the mistaken notion that good is merely the absence of doing that which is wrong. Not so! One is good not merely because he does no evil, but because he is actively working for what is good".Peter 3:11 Let him eschew evil, and do good. James 4:17 Therefore to him that knoweth to do good, and doeth it not, to him it is sin. *Quote by Wayne Greeson* http://www.padfield.com/1997/goodmen.html
>
> Matthew 25:30 And cast ye the unprofitable servant into outer darkness: there shall be weeping and gnashing of teeth?

2

Education

Some people say our public schools are not performing well. I disagree with that. I give our public schools an A+ rating. For dumbing down America. Let's look at the evidence to see if I'm right.

I believe it is safe to say that most, if not all, of our local and national legislators, and most, if not all, local and federal judges, were educated by our secular public schools and secular colleges and universities.

Let's look at the US debt—over $18 trillion. That is more than $57,000 per citizen and $154,000 per taxpayer. I only looked at about ten states, and the debt runs from over $3,000 to $15,000 per citizen. http://www.usdebtclock.org

Let's look at literacy. A 2012 education survey ranks US students thirty-sixth in the world for proficiency in math, reading, and science. That is a world rating of thirty-six out of sixty-five countries rated. http://nces.ed.gov/surveys/pisa/

How do we improve our nation's literacy?

Literacy is the byproduct of public education. The main agenda is indoctrination and social engineering.

"The hand that rocks the cradle is the hand that rules the world." —poet William Ross

Humanists, socialists, and communists are rocking the cradle by controlling the National Educational

Education

Association. The NEA has the monopoly on our public education by lobbing The Department of Education . I believe the NEA'S goal is to remove God from our society and establish an authoritarian statist government, where the state controls all economic and social affairs. Please read : ***NEA: Trojan Horse in American Education***
By Samuel Blumenfeld

How are Humanists, Socialists, and Communists meeting this goal?

They are doing it by cultivating our minds and establishing welfare communities with all ungodliness and unrighteousness, to cause a crisis of killing, rape, and stealing.

Do you remember this quote from our Declaration of Independence? "He has excited **domestic insurrections** amongst us, and has endeavoured to bring on the inhabitants of our frontiers, the **merciless Indian Savages**, whose known rule of warfare, is an undistinguished destruction of all ages, sexes and conditions."

"He has excited domestic insurrections amongst us," **race relations** to cause more killings, violence, and burning of our cities, and I believe we could replace merciless "**Indian Savages**" with "**Islamists terrorists**".

He "has endeavoured to bring on the inhabitants of our frontiers, the merciless [**Islamist terrorists**] Savages, whose known rule of warfare is an undistinguished destruction of all ages, sexes, and conditions."

Education

When you add the communist marketing of evil on our televisions, in movies, and in publishing, enforced by the America Civil Liberties Union, and then add Planned Parenthood's cultivating the minds of our children with sexual immorality and killing of unwanted human beings, now we have the makings of a crisis. But wait, there is one more…

> For the wrath of God is revealed from heaven against all ungodliness and unrighteousness of men, who hold the truth in unrighteousness.
> Romans 1:18

What is the wrath of God?

> Being filled with all unrighteousness, fornication, wickedness, covetousness, maliciousness; full of envy, murder, debate, deceit, malignity; whisperers.
> Romans 1: 29

I believe we will have the makings of a crisis big enough that most people will consent to a change in government.

What is the change?

It's the Second Amendment of our Constitution: "A well-regulated Militia, being necessary to the security of a free State, the right of the people to keep and bear Arms, shall not be infringed."

Notice the part that states, " being necessary to the security of a free State" I believe the majority of people will eventually vote to trade their freedom for security. Remember the 85% conformist, this includes christian church members.

Education

What do you think will happen to the Christians?

The old Serpent, known as the Devil, doesn't care if the Humanists, socialists, or communists rule, as long as the Christians don't.

> And while the children of Israel were in the wilderness, they found a man that gathered sticks upon the sabbath day. And they that found him gathering sticks brought him unto Moses and Aaron, and unto all the congregation. And they put him in ward, because it was not declared what should be done to him. And the Lord said unto Moses, The man shall be surely put to death: all the congregation shall stone him with stones without the camp. And all the congregation brought him without the camp, and stoned him with stones, and he died; as the Lord commanded Moses. Numbers 15:32–36

Did the Lord have him stoned for gathering sticks or for disobedience?

Do you believe the Lord is going to let the Christians by for disobedience?

What's happening to the Christians in the Middle East?

Let's see how our theological seminaries and Christian colleges are performing.

We have highly educated preachers, some with doctorate degrees, and most are well-educated, but do they have knowledge of the holy?

Education

I believe that most preachers minds have been corrupted from the simplicity that is in Christ; because we have legislators that are christian church members who lobby and vote for socialism and fund planned parenthood. We have christian church members who vote for these legislators. We have christian church members that doesn't know the difference between rights and goods. We have christian church members that doesn't know that socialism is stealing and stealing is against God's law "You shall not steal".

We have christian preachers, church members and local and state lesser magistrates who believe we are to obey all government laws: good or bad. If the churches would teach that rulers are to do good, but when rulers become bad and demand what God forbids and forbids what God demands they are not to be obeyed. "https://lessermagistrate.com/"
I believe the church is responsible for educating our children and sending them to secular government schools is like sending them to Satan for their education.

> Take heed therefore unto yourselves, and to all the flock, over which the Holy Ghost hath made you overseers, to feed the church of God, which He hath purchased with His own blood. Acts 20:28

I believe that our theological seminaries have been invaded by the Devil.

> 13 For such are false apostles, deceitful workers, transforming themselves into the apostles of Christ. 14 And no marvel; for Satan himself is transformed into an angel of light. 15 Therefore it is no great thing if his ministers also be

Education

transformed as the ministers of righteousness;
whose end shall be according to their works.
2 Corinthians 11:13 4

I believe that if the preachers, pastors and churches
were doing their job we would not have
government funded secular public schools.
Because of secular public schools we now have
secular colleges and universities.
Now America is becoming a Godless society.

I am the good shepherd: the good shepherd giveth
his life for the sheep. But he that is an hireling, and
not the shepherd, whose own the sheep are not,
seeth the wolf coming , and leaveth the sheep, and
fleeth : and the wolf catcheth them, and scattereth
the sheep. The hireling fleeth , because he is an
hireling, and careth not for the sheep.
John 10:11-13

3

How Should We Alter Our Government?

Before I share with you how I believe we should alter our government-controlled school system, I want to share with you my experience of education.

I was born in 1954 and went to school in the sixties. I was socially promoted from the fifth grade to the sixth grade and every year after that I was socially promoted up to the ninth grade. In eighth grade, I made all Fs and didn't take my semester exams. Ninth grade was high school, which was at another school. I failed ninth grade and went back the following year for about six weeks, and then dropped out of school and went to work.

When I turned eighteen, I wanted to join the Mississippi National Guard, but I needed a high-school diploma. I took the GED test, passed it, and joined the Guard. I got married, and my paw-in-law taught me how to weld well enough to get a job where he worked. After a couple of years, I kept saying to myself, "There has to be a better way."

I decided to go to school and study electronics. When it came time to register, the instructor asked me what math I had taken. I told him I'd failed general math. He asked me about algebra, trigonometry, and geometry. I told him I'd never taken those courses. He told me I needed to go back home, that I was wasting my time and money. I told him I had the time and money. He said he couldn't stop me from taking the course.

How Should We Alter Our Government?

On the first day of class, the instructor gave a math test. When he saw our test scores, he was very angry and threw the blackboard eraser against the wall and said, "Elementary." We didn't know how to even work common fractions. Of twenty-three students, two of us had GEDs. I could work common fractions, until it became difficult to find the least common denominator.

I did not know anything about algebra, so I developed a three-foot rule. If I got within three feet of someone, I asked if they knew anything about algebra. Most said no, and those who tried to help me said, "Move the known terms on one side of the equal sign and change the sign, and keep the unknown term on the other side of the equal sign."

I asked, "Why?"

They said, "I don't know, just do it."

I could not find anyone who could tell me *why*, and I was not smart enough to figure it out. I was about to drop out of school, but I found a used math book for fifty cents at the college bookstore. The name of the book was *Mathematics for Technicians*, by Edward M. Tronaas. If not for that book, I would have had to drop out of school.

I made a B in algebra, an A in trigonometry, and a C in English. I had a 3.4 grade point average, and I worked eight hours a night and forty hours a week. I took twelve and thirteen credit hours a semester. I only took math, electronics, and technical writing, and I took English during summer school. There were twenty-three students in the beginning, and eleven or twelve of us finished the electronics program.

How Should We Alter Our Government?

I thought the high-school graduates would have left me way behind, but I found myself helping them. I worked with one particular high-school grad, teaching him how to add and subtract measurements. The point I'm trying to get across is that teachers with degrees taught these students who did not acquire basic math skills.

How should we alter our school system?

- We should get the government out of education.

- We should get the NEA out of our schools.

- Parents are responsible for their children's education and should come up with a way to educate their children without the government's involvement.

- The church should be doing the educating.

- I believe the only requirement for a teacher to teach, is to pass a proficiency test in the subject to be taught and the ability to teach.

- There should not be time limits to move to the next grade level.

- When a student meets the requirement for twelfth-grade equivalence, he or she can move on to a vocational, technical, or academic education.

- We should phase out government funding of schools.

How Should We Alter Our Government?

• The people should—and I believe *will*—volunteer to pay for education. Nature's God can only bless volunteer giving.

If people who have a desire to teach were to study *As a Man Thinketh*, by James Allen; *Unlimited Power and Awaken the Giant Within*, by Anthony Robbins; *The Psychology of Persuasion*, by Kevin Hogan; and *How to Solve Problems and Prevent Trouble*, by Richard W. Wetherill, they could become masters of persuasion.

It's been said that the art of leadership is to get a person to *want* to do. When a person wants to do something, it's hard to stop him from doing it. I believe the biggest obstacle in teaching is getting students to want to learn.

So why should we alter the control of our schools?

• It's a strategic blunder to our national defense to allow one organization to control our schools. "The hand that rocks the cradle is the hand that rules the world." —poet William Ross

• It's not right to allow our children to be indoctrinated with ungodliness.

• Our children deserve to be educated to a high standard of literacy.

• Being thirty-sixth out of sixty-five countries in literacy is a standard that needs to be corrected. 2012 http://nces.ed.gov/surveys/pisa/

• Churches should be doing the teaching.

How Should We Alter Our Government?

Whom we preach, warning every man, and
teaching every man in all wisdom; that we may
present every man perfect in Christ Jesus.
Colossians 1:28

**What part of "all wisdom" could we better
understand?**

What else needs altering?

We need to alter our archaic English legal system,
because it provides so much opportunity for corruption.

An theatlantic.com article titled "America's English-
Style Legal System Evolved to Conceal Truth, Not
Reveal It" "The civil adversarial system that developed
over centuries in England, and later spread to the U.S.
and other colonies, might not work as well as a truth-
seeking system."

In the adversarial system where one wins and one loses,
it's tempting to lie, cheat, or cover up. In our ungodly and
unrighteous society, do you want to depend on lawyers'
moral values for your freedom? I have read that most
cases are settled out of court through plea bargaining,
which should not be allowed. We should seek the truth.
Read *A Case for Christ*, by Lee Strobel; *Tyranny with
Good Intentions*, by Paul Craig Roberts and Lawrence M.
Stratton; and *Good-bye America*, by JonathanWest, and
do an Internet search for " truth-seeking legal system."

I know of a guy, on his third DUI, who put $7,000 in
cash into his lawyer's hands: because he couldn't walk
straight he failed his sobriety test and his lawyer got him
off on account of he had bad knees.

How Should We Alter Our Government?

Is this justice?

Is it justice for him?

Is it justice for society?

"Luis Fernando Parada with 4 prior DUI convictions was charged with second degree murder, DUI Gross Vehicular Manslaughter and Driving on a suspended license and sentenced to 27.5 years' incarceration for killing Ryan Kyle Smith." (Source: madd.org)

Perhaps Parada has a wife and children.

Is this justice for the family of the accused?

With four prior DUIs, Parada's legal defense must have cost quite a bit. It seems that Parada has no consideration for himself, his family, or anyone else's well-being. We see that our justice system, lawyers, and judges may have no consideration for anyone but themselves. Parada's wife and children might have gotten more punishment than Parada did.

Should the family of the accused be punished for his behavior?

This is what our *in*justice system is doing, and we call this justice.

"We the People of the United States, in Order to form a more perfect Union, establish Justice, insure domestic Tranquility..."

How Should We Alter Our Government?

I have read it costs approximately $129 a day to keep people in prison.

What is the cost in dollars?

Parada was sentenced to 27.5 years; multiply that by 365 days, times $129.04 per day, and the total is $1,295,239.

What is the price of pain and anger of family and friends?

Not much is mentioned about the cost of the pain and suffering of the emotionally injured.

What about the accused?

Is leniency good for him?

Maybe it was just good for the lawyers. We see Parada's license was suspended.

Did a suspended license stop the accused from driving?

What should we do to correct the justice system?

"Singapore corporal punishment is used as a crime deterrent. Research from the *Los Angeles Times* article, "Singapore Justice System Gives US Examples for Thought," looked at the small city state of Singapore (where corporal punishment is legal) and Los Angeles (in the United States where it is not), with their roughly equal population of 3.5 million and found a striking crime differences. In 1993, fifty-eight murders, eighty rapes, 1,008 robberies and approx. thirty-one hundred car thefts were reported in Singapore. Los Angeles Police Department statistics for the same time period showed

How Should We Alter Our Government?

eleven hundred homicides, 1,855 rapes, 39,227 robberies and approx. sixty-six thousand car thefts. We as Americans should take a lesson from Singapore and enact new legislation instituting a new form of justice that is, corporal punishment."

We see that Los Angeles had about nineteen times more murders, about twenty-three times more rapes, about thirty-nine times more robberies, and about twenty-one times more car thefts.

The national center on Addiction and Substance abuse at Columbia University tells us that 80% of the adults in United States prisons are there because of criminal activity linked to drug and alcohol abuse.

According to The national center on Addiction and Substance Abuse at Columbia University each American paid $277 per year to deal with substance abuse and Addiction and $10 a year for prevention and treatment.

"One in 38 adult Mississippians is either behind bars or under correctional supervision; in 1982 the figure was 1 in 105 adults." (Source: alec.org)

Lawyers and judges have no incentive to stop the drug abuse, because defending the drug abusers is how the lawyers earn their living, and judges may be defending drug abusers if the judges loses their judge position. Cities and counties take in thousands of dollars in drug trade–fortified money, so there is no incentive to stop the drug abuse. Most legislators are under the power of Satan and have demonic blinders on, it seems to me they have no desire to stop the drug and substance abuse. They will want to rehabilitate and be loving and give leniency and I don't believe leniency is working.

Anthony Robbins author of *Unlimited Power* says we don't move away from real pain we move away from what leads to pain . If we would link massive amount pain to any behavior we would avoid it it at all cost.

All we need to do is to have the punishment harsh enough so people would link massive amount of pain to using illegal drugs and substance abuse

So whose fault is it?

I believe it is the pastors and preachers, who are supposed to shepherd the flock.

> Wherefore, I take you to record this day, that I am pure from the blood of all men. For I have not shunned to declare unto you all the counsel of God. Take heed therefore unto yourselves, and to all the flock, over the which the Holy Ghost hath made you overseers, to feed the church of God, which He hath purchased with His own blood. Acts 20:26

4

What Should We Do?

We should follow God's way.

> For rulers are not a terror to good works, but to the evil. Wilt thou then not be afraid of the power? do that which is good, and thou shalt have praise of the same: For he is the minister of God to thee for good. But if thou do that which is evil, be afraid; for he beareth not the sword in vain: for he is the minister of God, a revenger to execute wrath upon him that doeth evil. Romans 13:3–4

We see that the rulers are to "execute wrath upon him that doeth evil." It doesn't say to execute wrath upon his family, too.

What is God's way?

God's way is discipline.

> For whom the Lord loveth he chasteneth, and scourgeth every son whom he receiveth. Hebrews 12:6 Correction is grievous unto him that forsaketh the way: and he that hateth reproof shall die. Proverbs 15:10 A servant will not be corrected by words: for though he understand he will not answer. Proverbs 29:19 Foolishness is bound in the heart of a child; but the rod of correction shall drive it far from him. Proverbs 22:15 Withhold not correction from the child: for if thou beatest him with the rod, he shall not die. Proverbs 23:13 A whip for the horse, a bridle for the ass, and a rod

What Should We Do?

for the fool's back. Proverbs 26:3 And when he
had made a scourge of small cords, he drove them
all out of the temple. John 2:15

Jesus used a scourge of small cords.

What is preventing us from doing the same as Jesus?

**Do you believe Satan's ministers of righteousness are
preventing us from using corporal punishment?**

I don't. Christians are preventing us from using corporal
punishment, because we are doing nothing to change our
unjust legal system to a truth-seeking system and one of
corporal punishment.

> Be not deceived: evil communications corrupt
> good manners. Awake to righteousness, and sin
> not; for some have not the knowledge of God. I
> speak this to your shame. 1 Corinthians 15:33–34

> For my thoughts are not your thoughts, neither are
> your ways my ways, saith the Lord. Isaiah 55:8

How should we change our law?

• We should establish a universal law.

• We should not cause harm or unnecessary risk of harm
to people, property, or the environment.

• We should establish a Truth Seeking Council System to
decide what a necessary risk is and determine the
punishment for causing harm or unnecessary risk of harm
to people, property, or the environment.

What Should We Do?

• We should eliminate monetary fines. People should not be able to pay their way out of causing harm to others.

• We should stop all liability insurance, product liability, and malpractice insurance. People should insure themselves and their property.

• If anyone causes harm or unnecessary risk of harm to people, property, or the environment, a root-cause analysis should be done to determine the cause and what can be done to prevent it from happening again. If you don't want to be in fear, then do what is right.

> For rulers are not a terror to good works, but to the evil. Wilt thou then not be afraid of the power? do that which is good, and thou shalt have praise of the same: For he is the minister of God to thee for good. But if thou do that which is evil, be afraid; for he beareth not the sword in vain: for he is the minister of God, a revenger to execute wrath upon him that doeth evil. Romans 13:3–4

We see that the rulers are "to execute wrath upon him that doeth evil." It doesn't say to execute wrath upon others. It says "to execute wrath upon him that doeth evil." Companies, corporations, and hospitals are not people—they are made up of people and people run them, so people are responsible for harm to other people, property, or the environment.

Lawsuits mostly benefit lawyers and insurance companies. The more the insurance company pays out for settlements, the more we as consumers pay for it. The companies are in business to earn money—until the

What Should We Do?

premiums cost so much that policy holders and customers can't pay the costs.

What happens next?

Satan's ministers of righteousness, our legislators, take control and fix the crisis. If spiritual wickedness in high places takes control, no good will ever come from it. Remember that it takes a crisis to get the people to consent to change. That's why we have ObamaCare, the Affordable Care Act health care reform law.

> 6 But brother goeth to law with brother, and that before the unbelievers. 7 Now therefore there is utterly a fault among you, because ye go to law one with another. Why do ye not rather take wrong ? why do ye not rather suffer yourselves to be defrauded ? 8 Nay, ye do wrong , and defraud , and that your brethren. 9 Know ye not that the unrighteous shall not inherit the kingdom of God? Be not deceived : neither fornicators, nor idolaters, nor adulterers, nor effeminate, nor abusers of themselves with mankind, 10 Nor thieves, nor covetous, nor drunkards, nor revilers, nor extortioners, shall inherit * the kingdom of God. Corinthians 6:6–8

We are suing ourselves out of a quality of life and standard of living. We are working for lawyers and insurance companies. When costs of goods go up, we need higher salaries to survive. Then the costs of goods go up again, until it is no longer practical to produce goods in the United States.

What Should We Do?

Most companies provide workers' compensation and personal medical insurance. If responsibility for their own safety, and the safety of others, is placed on employees, in the event anyone gets injured on or off the job, a root-cause analysis should be done to determine the cause. If anyone causes harm or unnecessary risk of harm to others or himself, it should be determined if someone ought to be punished, because when a person gets injured it costs everyone. We should have one medical insurance policy that provides coverage on and off the job. If anyone gets injured on the job, he or she could handle it just like an off-the-job injury. Premiums should be based on risk factors on and off the job, such as with high-risk sports.

Product Liability Insurance

We should do away with product liability insurance and hold the people responsible for doing what is right. As long as products meet manufacturing standards and people do what is right, no one should have to fear. Only the evildoers should fear. The consumer should determine if the product will meet his or her safety standard and if it should fail the consumer should determine if they need to insured it for lost caused by failure.

Automobile Liability Insurance

We should do away with automobile liability insurance, because we are exposed to more liability than most normal people can pay. If you have a $100,000 liability insurance policy and caused $250,000.00 worth of damage your insurance company would pay the

What Should We Do?

$100,000.00 and you would owe $150,000.00. Would you be able to pay that?

How much is enough—$1 million? $2 million? $3 million?

I know of a construction firm that caused more than $1 million in damage. The firm's insurance company paid $1 million, and the construction company paid monthly payments for about five years to cover the damages. Do you carry just the minimum requirements or just enough to cover what you have to lose? You can't get something from people who have nothing to lose. People who have nothing to lose have the opportunity to get something from the people who do have something to lose. This is not equal justice but *in*justice.

A friend of mine was permanently disabled by a drunk driver and lives with constant pain. The driver, driving a borrowed truck, was killed. Neither the driver nor the truck owner had insurance—nor any assets to lose. If not for my friend's uninsured motorist insurance, he wouldn't have gotten any compensation. We all know riding in an automobile is a necessary risk. When a driver knows he could be punished for causing an incident and that the punishment could range from community service to lashing, flogging, or even the death sentence, he will become a safer driver. Safer driving means fewer incidences, and fewer incidences means lower premiums for insurance.

What Should We Do?

Medical Malpractice Insurance

"The average malpractice premium in Minnesota is estimated at $8,500 while the average premium in Florida is estimated at $79,000! Why such an astronomical difference? Do Florida doctors make more mistakes than those in Minnesota? Of course not. In fact, Florida physicians are probably less risk tolerant and pressured to practice medicine more defensively. There are approximately 4,000 emergency physicians in Florida. If they were to convert their insurance to a Minnesota carrier, they would save $70,000 per doc for a total of $280 million! Where does this $280 million come from and where does it go? EPs in both states are paid approximately the same. However, Medicare spending is $6,911 per capita in Minneapolis and $13,824 in Miami. Put another way, each year we taxpayers make a $280 million donation to Florida's trial lawyers. The bottom line is this: It's not about justice. It's not about good medicine. It's about money." (Source: epmonthly.com)

I disagree with taxpayers making a $280 million donation to Florida's trial lawyers. Taxes are collected to pay for government services and to secure our unalienable rights. This $280 million of "stolen money" was used to pay for goods. If I were to rob you and use the money to pay for someone's insurance premiums, I would still be charged with robbery. In God's law, it's stealing.

When someone gets harmed by someone with nothing to lose, the harmed person cannot get anything. He can only file charges: if the person is convicted of misconduct he should get punished. If the person who files a malpractice lawsuit were to harm someone else, do you believe he

44

could pay the person he harmed $1 million or $2 million? What would he do if he were injured by another person who had nothing to lose? You don't get to choose who injures you. Most of the time, you get to choose your doctor. The ruling authority is a revenger to execute wrath upon him that doeth evil, not a revenger to execute wrath on everyone. Lawsuits cost everyone.

What does equal justice mean?

THE SUPREME COURT

"It has long been my opinion, and I have never shrunk from its expression, the germ of dissolution of our federal government is in the constitution of the federal judiciary; an irresponsible body (for impeachment is scarcely a scarecrow) working like gravity by night and by day, gaining a little to-day and a little to-morrow, and advancing its noiseless step like a thief, over the field of jurisdiction, until all shall be usurped from the States, and the government of all be consolidated into one. To this I am opposed; because, when all government, domestic and foreign, in little as in great things, shall be drawn to Washington as the centre of all power, it will render powerless the checks provided of one government on another, and will become as venal and oppressive as the government from which we separated." —Thomas Jefferson

> For we wrestle not against flesh and blood, but against principalities, against powers, against the rulers of the darkness of this world, against spiritual wickedness in high places. Ephesians 6:12

What Should We Do?

We can clearly see the spiritual wickedness at work in the Supreme Court.

How can we better the Supreme Court?

"All authority is delegated and no man or woman holds their office autonomously. This authority received in office is delegated by God and thus, all those in authority stand accountable to God. This is why the practice of the church historically has been—when the State commands that which God forbids or forbids that which God commands, we have a duty to obey God rather than man. The Bible clearly teaches this principle and we now live in the midst of a statist, slave-like people where such thinking has long been forgotten."
(Source: lessermagistrate.com)

"We hold these truths to be self-evident, that all men are created equal, that they are endowed by their Creator with certain unalienable Rights, that among these are Life, Liberty and the pursuit of Happiness.—That to secure these rights, Governments are instituted among Men, deriving their just powers from the consent of the governed,—That whenever any Form of Government becomes destructive of these ends, it is the Right of the People to alter or to abolish it, and to institute new Government, laying its foundation on such principles and organizing its powers in such form, as to them shall seem most likely to effect their Safety and Happiness"

We see that whenever any form of government becomes destructive to these ends, it is the right of the people to alter or to abolish it and to institute new government.

What Should We Do?

What is preventing us from encouraging our legislators to abolish the Supreme Court?

The Christians are doing nothing to unite together and if christians don't unite together and start following God's way when our government demands what God forbids and forbids what God demands we will lose all of our freedom.

What do the Christians control?

Nothing! We are like slaves, doing nothing to protect our freedom.

> But be ye doers of the word, and not hearers only, deceiving your own selves. James 1:22

> Even so faith, if it hath not works, is dead, being alone. Yea, a man may say, Thou hast faith, and I have works: shew me thy faith without thy works, and I will shew thee my faith by my works. Thou believest that there is one God; thou doest well: the devils also believe, and tremble. But wilt thou know, O vain man, that faith without works is dead? James 2:17–20

AMERICAN BAR ASSOCIATION (ABA)

We should stop the monopoly on legal practice. We should be able to hire legal secretaries to handle minor contracts, land deeds, and other legal work, and all contracts should be written in plain English, not legal terminology.

What Should We Do?

AMERICAN MEDICAL ASSOCIATION (AMA)

We should stop the AMA's monopoly on medical practice, because it is my inalienable right to choose my doctor. If I want to choose Dr. Quack, Dr. Voodoo, or any other doctor, it's my right.

What right does the AMA have to stop me from choosing my medical practitioner?

How much harm do you believe allopath doctors do and get by with?

In order to be a doer, you have to *want* to. When a person wants to do something, it's hard to stop her from doing what she wants to do.

Do you know of a baby or toddler who lays her head on your shoulder, puts her arms around your neck, and goes to sleep? She has faith in you, trusting you will protect and love her. Will you find enough love to shed a tear for her future? If you can find enough love to pray with tears and a broken heart for her future, asking God for wisdom, understanding, and a worthwhile purpose in life, or give you death, then I believe He will remove the demonic blinders so you can see and hear things differently than you have seen and heard them before. This time, what you see and hear will go also to your heart and not only your head. Be warned! Your heart might be broken many times, because when you share what you see and feel with your family and friends, they might not be interested. Don't forget that you, too, might have been skeptical before the demonic blinders were removed.

5

Islam

Should the Islam religion be protected under the First Amendment?

"Congress shall make no law respecting an establishment of religion, or prohibiting the free exercise thereof; or abridging the freedom of speech, or of the press; or the right of the people peaceably to assemble, and to petition the government for a redress of grievances." —First Amendment to the Constitution of the United States of America

PREAMBLE OF THE US CONSTITUTION

"We the People of the United States, in Order to form a more perfect Union, establish Justice, insure domestic Tranquility, provide for the Common defense, promote the General Welfare, and secure the Blessings of Liberty to ourselves and our Posterity, do ordain and establish this Constitution for the United States of America."

The preamble of the Constitution states its purpose and intent.

Should we reference the preamble of the Constitution when interpreting the Bill of Rights?

Let's reference each item of our Preamble to the teaching of the Koran—the source of Islam's core belief.

• To form a more perfect union

• Establish justice

- Ensure domestic tranquility

- Provide for the common defense

- Promote the general welfare

- Secure the blessings of liberty to ourselves and our posterity

Does the teaching of the Koran—the source of Islam's core belief—meet the purpose and intent of our Bill of Rights?

Below are some Surahs from The Koran chapter and verse.

Because of copyright law, I'm not publishing the verses.

You should get and read the *The Koran* (Penguin Classics) by N. J. Dawood and *The Complete Infidel's Guide to the Koran* by Robert Spencer Kindle Edition http://www.amazon.com

Koran (Penguin Classics) by N. J. Dawood Kindle Edition http://www.amazon.com

Free online translation http://corpus.quran.com/translation.jsp

48:29, 08:038, 8:12, 066:009, 018:001, 005:72, 005:73, 2:178, 3:118, 5:51, 98:7, 3:19, 048:023, 3:28

Is this what you want in America?

May we yell, "Fire!" in a crowded theater when there is no fire?

Islam

Islam goes beyond the First Amendment. Any nation that will allow Islam to flourish is doomed to be an Islamic nation or be terrorized.

Any nation's people that don't read and understand Islam will become an Islamic nation or will be terrorized.

History produces evidence that no other religion can live peacefully alongside Islam—it's against the religion Islam, but Islam can live peacefully alongside other religions until Muslims get strong enough to take control. If we continue to choose to look the other way and do nothing, our freedom will be taken away and given to the Muslims.

Government, culture, and religion are combined to form the Islam religion. In order for Muslims to practice their religion, they will want to have their own government. When they get their own government in their community, they will be happy for a little while but not for long. It will be just like the pilgrims' coming to America and pushing the Native American Indians off the land. Please read *"Fast Facts for false doctrine"*
by Ron Carson/Ed Decker

I worked in the countries of Saudi Arabia and Qatar for about twelve years and had no issues with the people. We got along well, we laugh, talk, drank coffee and tea together. This muslim had been helping me learn some arabic words for a while and then the subject of the Koran came up and I ask him did he know about the Koran, he said yes. I ask him about the Surahs "Believers, do not make friends with any but your own people." (3:118) "Believers, take neither the Jews nor the Christians for your friends." (5:51) and from that point on he had nothing to do with me. This is the power of belief. I'm glad I didn't show him this surah "Muhammad is God's apostle. Those who follow him are ruthless to the unbelievers but merciful to one another." (48:29) He wasn't ruthless to me in any way, he just didn't talk to me anymore.

The point I'm getting at is they can be peace loving people today, but if and when some charismatic spiritual leader and the power of Satan get to them, they can become terrorists tomorrow. I'm not talking about being terrorists to just Americans. I'm talking about to other muslims as well. I was working with a muslim when the suicide bomber blown up the mosque in Saudi Arabia. He showed me photos of the mosque and the bomber's body blown into. That happen in the city he lived in. You should read the Koran for yourself.

If you would read the Koran you would see that the god of the Koran is not the God of the Holy Bible.

If the Native American Indians had it to do over again, do you believe they would do something differently?

Every Christian church in America should have a mission to evangelize the Muslims. We have the opportunity to share the Gospels here in America. It's against the law to evangelize in Islamic countries.

> Jesus sent Paul: "To open their eyes, and to turn them from darkness to light, and from the power of Satan unto God, that they may receive forgiveness of sins, and inheritance among them which are sanctified by faith that is in me." Acts 26:18

6

Book Recommendations

Jesus Is Involved in Politics! Why Aren't You? Why Isn't Your Church?

By Neil Mammen

Learn more about *Jesus Is Involved in Politics!* at noblindfaith.com.

Mind Siege: The Battle for Truth in the New Millennium

By Tim LaHaye and David Noebel

If you read *Mind Siege*, you will see why you need to also read *Jesus Is Involved in Politics!*, featured above.

The Family Under Siege: What the New Social Engineers Have in Mind for You and Your Children

By George Grant

The Tyranny of Good Intentions: How Prosecutors and Law Enforcement Are Trampling the Constitution in the Name of Justice

By Paul Craig Roberts and Lawrence M. Stratton

The Case for Christ: A Journalist's Personal Investigation of the Evidence for Jesus

Book Recommendations

NEA: Trojan Horse in American Education

By Samuel Blumenfeld

Good-bye America?

By Jonathan West

The Doctrine of the Lesser Magistrates: A Proper Resistance to Tyranny and a Repudiation of Unlimited Obedience to Civil Government

By Pastor Matthew J. Trewhella

lessermagistrate.com

Praying Effectively for the Lost

By Lee E. Thomas pelministries.org

The Koran (Penguin Classics) by N. J. Dawood

The Complete Infidel's Guide to the Koran

by Robert Spencer

Spiritual Warfare
Christians, Demonization, and Deliverance
by Dr. Karl I. Payne

Book Recommendations

RECOMMENDED ARTICLE

"When Good Men Do Nothing"

By Wayne Greeson http://www.padfield.com/1997/goodmen.html

RECOMMENDED DOCUMENTARY FILMS

Agenda: Grinding America Down

agendadocumentary.com

This is serious and a true story.

The Isaiah 9:10 Judgment: Is There an Ancient Mystery That Foretells America's Future? http://superstore.wnd.com/

DVD *IndoctriNation: Public Schools and the Decline of Christianity in America*

indoctrinationmovie.com/film

ABOUT THE AUTHOR

My name is Jerry Dedeaux.

Occupation: Maintenance Electrician

Why this book?

I asked God to give me a worthwhile purpose in life or give me death. I asked God why there is so much evil in America when we have so many churches.

Not long after, I was cleaning out my bookcase and found a book titled *The Battle for the Mind: A Subtle Warfare*, by Dr. Tim LaHaye. I don't know where I got the book; all I know is that it was a used book, and it stood out and I had a desire to read it. It answered a lot of questions I had. Not long after that, my daughter bought me a book from camp titled *The Family Under Siege: What the New Social Engineers Have in Mind for You and Your Children*, by George Grant.

I became aware of what was happening, as though my eyes had been opened, and I have a conviction to share this information with others and preach to preachers. I have read a lot of other books, but the one I'm trying to encourage pastors and church members to read is *Jesus Is*

ABOUT THE AUTHOR

Involved in Politics! Why Aren't You? Why Isn't Your Church? If we don't get involved in politics, we are going to lose our freedom of religion, freedom of speech, and other freedoms.

When I read the Bible, some verses just touched me as if I'd become aware of the meanings.

Take away the dross from silver, and there shall come forth a vessel for the finer. Take away the wicked from before the king, and his throne will be established in righteousness. Proverbs 25:4

When the righteous are in authority, the people rejoice, but when a wicked man rules, the people groan. Proverbs 29:2

And this quote by politician Sam Ervin struck me:

"If men and women of capacity refuse to take part in politics and government, they condemn themselves, as well as the people, to the punishment of living under bad government."

But be ye doers of the word, and not hearers only, deceiving your own selves. James 1:22

www.jerrydedeaux.com

57

www.ingramcontent.com/pod-product-compliance
Lightning Source LLC
Chambersburg PA
CBHW030531290526
45786CB00004B/1680